A Little Indulgence

SPIRITS

Printed in the United States of America
by G&R Publishing Co.

Distributed By:

507 Industrial Street
Waverly, IA 50677

ISBN-13: 978-1-56383-218-5
ISBN-10: 1-56383-218-6
Item #6204

Ever wonder why hard alcohol and mixed drinks are called "spirits"? Some believe the name derives from the process by which alcohol is created. Alcohol boils at a lower temperature than water, there-fore, the still used to create the beverage, if maintained at a proper degree, will cause the alcohol to evaporate into mist or "spirits". Only water and mash are left behind. The still cools down the vapor, causing it to condense into a liquid.

Another theory is that alcohol, once consumed, lowers the energetic field of your personality. With all guards let down, "spirits" can then enter the body. This is why people, under the influence of spirits, will sometimes act differently than they would under normal conditions. Once the alcohol wears off, the level of consciousness rises and spirits leave the body.

Spirits are often defined as any distilled liquor containing much alcohol, such as rum, whiskey, brandy and gin. Therefore, the distinction is made from wine and malt liquors. However spirits came to be named as such, it remains true that spirits and drinks containing spirits are widely popular throughout the world. Spirits are used to enhance celebration, as in the case of parties, special occasions and weddings. They are used to calm the nerves or warm the body. Some say creating mixed drinks with spirits is an art that talented bartenders each blend with their own style. It is apparent, though, that spirits have placed their own mark on history and left a different taste in everyone's mouth. So shake up a martini, mix yourself a cocktail or pour a sweet brandy old-fashioned, and turn the page to discover more about the wild world of spirits...

COSMOPOLITAN
Makes 2 servings

3 oz. vodka
1 oz. cointreau
2 tsp. fresh lime juice

3 oz. cranberry juice
Twists of lime for garnish

In a cocktail shaker filled with ice, combine vodka, cointreau, fresh lime juice and cranberry juice. Shake vigorously and strain mixture into chilled martini glasses. Garnish each serving with a twist of lime peel.

MAI TAI

Makes 2 servings

3 oz. dark rum
1 oz. orange curacao
1 oz. crème de noyaux
1 oz. lime juice

Dash of grenadine
4 maraschino cherries
   for garnish

In a cocktail shaker filled with ice, combine dark rum, orange curacao, crème de noyaux, lime juice and grenadine. Shake vigorously and strain mixture into hurricane glasses filled with ice. Garnish each serving with two maraschino cherries.

GLASSWARE FOR SPIRITS

Part of the fun of serving spirits and mixed drinks is the presentation. The correct glassware is an essential part of the process and can enhance the quality and appearance of the drink.

HIGHBALL GLASS (8 OR 12 OUNCES)

A highball is used to serve any drink that is a concoction of alcohol and a mixer. Highball glasses are clear, simple and have no stem. Serve rum and coke, scotch and soda, bourbon and water, etc. in highball glasses.

LOWBALL GLASS (4 TO 9 OUNCES)

Also known as the rocks glass because they are used to serve many drinks with ice. This glass is appropriate for serving any stirred cocktail on the rocks. It is often popular to serve highball drinks in lowball glasses.

COCKTAIL GLASS (4 OUNCES)

Since cocktails are served without ice, it is appropriate to hold the glass by the stem so as not to warm the contents of the glass with your hands.

COLLINS GLASS (10 TO 14 OUNCES)

Originally created to serve a Tom Collins, this glass is used for various fizzy and tropical drinks. The glass is tall and round without a stem and is usually frosted or pebbled with a smooth rim.

MARTINI GLASS (4 OUNCES)

This glass is similar to the cocktail glass, though the bowl is slightly less tapered. The shape of the glass is perfect for cradling an olive.

MARGARITA GLASS (6 OUNCES)

These glasses have a unique double bowl. The wide upper rim of the glass allows for the drink to have a plentiful amount of salt or sugar, while the smaller inner bowl increases the impact of color from grenadine or liqueur.

SHOT GLASS (1 ½ OUNCES)

These tiny glasses, also called jiggers, were once used only to measure the amount of alcohol poured into a drink. It wasn't until the 1970's that bartenders started creating complex drinks served in shot glasses.

HOT TODDIE
Makes 2 servings

2 tsp. sugar, divided
2½ oz. brandy or bourbon, divided

2 C. boiling water, divided
Twists of orange or lemon peel for garnish

In 2 mugs, combine 1 teaspoon sugar and 1¼ ounces brandy or bourbon. Add 1 cup boiling water to each mug and mix lightly. Garnish each serving with a twist of orange or lemon peel.

HOMEMADE AMARETTO
Makes 3 cups

1 C. water
1 C. sugar
½ C. brown sugar

2 C. vodka
2 T. almond extract
2 tsp. vanilla

In a large saucepan over medium heat, combine water, sugar and brown sugar. Bring mixture to a boil, stirring frequently, until sugars are completely dissolved. Remove from heat and let mixture cool for 10 minutes. Add vodka, almond extract and vanilla and mix well. Funnel mixture into a bottle or jar and cover tightly with a sealed lid. Serve in a highball glass over ice or use in recipes calling for amaretto.

BAHAMA MAMA
Makes 1 serving

½ oz. rum
½ oz. coconut flavored rum
½ oz. grenadine
1 oz. orange juice

1 oz. pineapple juice
1 C. crushed ice
1 maraschino cherry
for garnish

In a blender, combine rum, coconut rum, grenadine, orange juice, pineapple juice and crushed ice. Process on high until mixture is slushy in consistency. Pour mixture into a cocktail glass and garnish with a maraschino cherry.

THE BEST PINA COLADAS

Makes 6 to 8 servings

1 (20 oz.) can sliced
  pineapple in juice
1 (15 oz.) can cream
  of coconut liqueur

3 C. ice cubes
¾ C. rum
8 maraschino cherries
  for garnish

Set aside two pineapple slices. In a blender, combine remaining pineapple slices in juice and cream of coconut liqueur. Process on high for 1 to 2 minutes, until well blended. Add ice cubes and rum and blend until ice cubes are crushed. Pour mixture into hurricane glasses. Cut each remaining pineapple slice into quarters. Slide one pineapple chunk and one maraschino cherry onto 8 skewers. Garnish each glass with a fruit skewer and serve.

BRANDY SLUSH
Makes 6 servings

¾ C. vodka
¾ C. brandy
1 (6 oz.) can frozen orange
juice concentrate, thawed
1 (12 oz.) can frozen
lemonade concentrate,
thawed

2 (10 oz.) jars maraschino
cherries
1 (32 oz.) bottle grapefruit
soda or ruby red Squirt
1 (1 liter) bottle lemon
lime soda

In a large freezer container, combine vodka, brandy, orange juice concentrate, lemonade concentrate, maraschino cherries and grapefruit soda. Mix well and cover tightly with a lid. Place mixture in freezer for 1 to 2 days. When ready to serve, using an ice cream scoop, scoop frozen mixture into six Collins glasses. Fill glasses with lemon lime soda. Mix lightly and serve.

MULLED RUM CIDER

Makes 12 to 16 servings

1 gallon apple cider
4 cinnamon sticks
1½ tsp. whole allspice
1 tsp. whole cloves
1 orange, sliced

1 lemon, sliced
1 C. rum
Twist of orange or lemon
  peel for garnish

In a large pot over high heat, combine cider, cinnamon sticks, allspice, whole cloves, orange slices and lemon slices. Bring mixture to a boil, stirring occasionally. Reduce heat to low, cover and let simmer for 45 minutes. Mix in rum and stir slightly. Using a slotted spoon, remove cinnamon sticks, whole allspice and whole cloves from mixture. To serve, ladle cider mixture into mugs and garnish each serving with an orange or lemon peel.

LEMON DROP
Makes 4 servings

4 oz. fresh lemon juice
2 oz. vodka
1 tsp. sugar
Crushed ice

1 lemon, sliced
4 sprigs fresh mint
  for garnish

In a cocktail shaker filled with ice, combine fresh lemon juice, vodka and sugar. Shake vigorously and strain mixture into chilled lowball glasses filled with crushed ice. Garnish each serving with a lemon slice and 1 sprig fresh mint.

LONG ISLAND ICED TEA

Makes 1 serving

1 (1½ oz.) jigger vodka
1 (1½ oz.) jigger gin
1 (1½ oz.) jigger rum
1 (1½ oz.) jigger triple sec

1 tsp. tequila
2 tsp. orange juice
2 oz. cola
1 lemon wedge for garnish

In a cocktail shaker filled with ice, combine vodka, gin, rum, triple sec and tequila. Shake vigorously and add orange juice and cola. Shake slightly and strain mixture into a chilled Collins glass. Garnish with a lemon wedge.

FROZEN MUDSLIDES
Makes 4 servings

4 C. crushed ice
2 (1½ oz.) jiggers vodka
2 (1½ oz.) jiggers coffee
flavored liqueur
2 (1½ oz.) jiggers Irish
crème liqueur

2 T. chocolate syrup
½ C. whipped topping
for garnish

In a blender, combine crushed ice, vodka, coffee flavored liqueur and Irish crème liqueur. Drizzle chocolate syrup over ingredients in blender. Process on high until well blended and smooth. Pour into Collins glasses and garnish each serving with a dollop of whipped topping.

BLOODY MARY

Makes 1 serving

1½ oz. vodka
Dash of Worcestershire
   sauce
Dash of Tabasco sauce
Dash of lime juice

Pinch of celery salt
Pinch of pepper
1 C. tomato juice
1 stalk celery with leaves

In a Collins glass filled with ice cubes, pour vodka. Add Worcestershire sauce, Tabasco sauce, lime juice, celery salt and pepper. Mix lightly with a long spoon and add tomato juice. Garnish with a celery stalk.

DIRTY MARTINI
Makes 2 servings

12 oz. vodka
Dash of dry vermouth

2 oz. liquid from olive jar
8 stuffed olives for garnish

In a cocktail shaker filled with ice, combine vodka, dry vermouth and olive juice. Shake vigorously and strain mixture into chilled martini glasses. Garnish each serving with four stuffed olives.

CHOCOLATE MARTINI
Makes 2 servings

4 oz. chocolate flavored
  liqueur
3 oz. vodka

½ oz. grated semisweet
  chocolate for garnish

In a cocktail shaker filled with ice, combine chocolate liqueur and vodka. Shake vigorously and strain mixture into chilled martini glasses. Garnish each serving with grated chocolate.

LIME MARGARITAS
ON THE ROCKS
Makes 8 servings

2 C. sour mix
1 C. tripe sec
1½ C. tequila
⅓ C. Grand Marnier

2 limes, quartered
Salt for garnish
Ice cubes

In a blender, combine sour mix, triple sec, tequila and Grand Marnier. Process on high until well combined. Dip the rim of eight margarita glasses in salt. Fill glasses with ice and pour margarita mixture over ice in each glass. Garnish each serving with a lime wedge.

BLENDED STRAWBERRY MARGARITAS

Makes 4 servings

4 C. ice cubes
6 oz. tequila
2 oz. triple sec
8 oz. frozen sliced
  strawberries in syrup

4 oz. frozen limeade
  concentrate, thawed
Powdered sugar for garnish

In a blender, place ice. Process on high until ice is crushed and add tequila and triple sec. Add strawberries in syrup and limeade. Blend on high for 30 seconds, or until mixture is smooth. Dip the rim of 4 margarita glasses in powdered sugar and pour blended mixture evenly into each glass.

" *Always do sober what you said you'd do drunk. That will teach you to keep your mouth shut.* "

Ernest Hemmingway

HOMEMADE IRISH CRÈME LIQUEUR

Makes 4 servings

3 eggs
1 (14 oz.) can sweetened
   condensed milk
3 T. chocolate syrup
2½ T. instant coffee granules

1 (16 oz.) bottle liquid
   non-dairy creamer
1 tsp. vanilla
1 tsp. almond extract
1¼ C. brandy

In a blender, combine eggs, sweetened condensed milk, chocolate syrup and instant coffee granules. Process on high for 3 minutes. Add liquid creamer, vanilla, almond extract and brandy. Blend for 12 minutes. Place mixture in refrigerator overnight. Before serving, strain liquid through cheesecloth, discarding any solids. Serve in highball glasses over ice or use in recipes calling for Irish crème liqueur.

Warning: Eating raw eggs is not recommended for pregnant women, the elderly and the sick because there is a risk that eggs may be contaminated with salmonella bacteria.

RASPBERRY KISS

Makes 1 serving

1 (1½ oz.) jibber raspberry
vodka

1 (1½ oz.) jigger strawberry
vodka

1 oz. lemon lime soda

1 (1½ oz.) jigger Chambord

Twist of orange for garnish

In a cocktail shaker filled with ice, combine raspberry vodka, strawberry vodka and lemon lime soda. Shake vigorously and strain mixture into a chilled cocktail glass. Pour Chambord slowly over top and garnish with a twist of orange peel.

THE ORIGINAL HURRICANE

Makes 1 serving

2 oz. light rum
2 oz. dark rum
2 oz. passion fruit juice
1 oz. orange juice
½ oz. lime juice

1 T. grenadine
1 maraschino cherry
for garnish
1 orange slice for garnish

In a cocktail shaker filled with ice, combine light rum, dark rum, passion fruit juice, orange juice, lime juice and grenadine. Shake vigorously and strain mixture into a chilled hurricane glass. Garnish with a maraschino cherry and an orange slice.

SPIRITS IN AMERICAN HISTORY

1870s

In 1874, a bartender at the Manhattan Club in New York invented "The Manhattan" at the request of Lady Randolph Churchill, the mother of Winston Churchill, who was throwing a party for the politician, Samuel J. Tilden.

1890s

The highball glass was invented in a St. Louis saloon for railroad workers who only had time for a quick drink. The glass was named after the ball placed on a high pole indicating it was time for railroad engineers to speed up.

1900s

Absinthe was one of the few socially acceptable drinks a woman could consume and it was often served in coffee houses.

1920s

In January of 1919 the 18th Amendment, which banned the manufacture, sale or transportation of intoxicating liquors, was added to the Constitution. The public

grew disenchanted with the law and underground saloons
became a booming business.

1930s

Though invented around 1900, the martini became
very popular in the 30s. FDR toasted the end of prohibition in 1933 with a Dirty Martini.

1940s

Trader Vic invented the Mai Tai in 1944 at his Hinky
Dinks restaurant. Mrs. Wright, a Tahitian patron, pro-
claimed, "Mai Tai, Roa Ae," after tasting the invention.
Her words translate to, "Out of this world, the best!"

1960s

JFK proclaimed the not-so-new Daiquiri as his favorite
drink, boosting its popularity throughout the decade. Frank
Sinatra enjoyed two fingers of Jack Daniels and water
served in an old-fashioned glass, rather than a highball.

1970s

Sweet cocktails were all the rage! The Pina Colada,
which was probably invented in 1954, became popular
during this decade.

BLUE HAWAIIAN
Makes 1 serving

1 oz. light rum
1 oz. blue curacao
2 oz. pineapple juice
1 oz. cream of coconut

1 maraschino cherry
  for garnish
1 pineapple wedge
  for garnish

In a blender, combine light rum, blue curacao, pineapple juice, cream of coconut and ice. Process on high speed until well blended. Pour into a Collins glass and garnish with a maraschino cherry and pineapple wedge.

HOLIDAY HOT COCOA

Makes 8 servings

1 C. nonfat dry milk
⅓ C. sugar
¼ C. cocoa powder
¼ C. powdered nondairy
  creamer
Pinch of salt

5 C. water
1 tsp. vanilla
½ C. rum
½ C. crème de cacao
8 miniature candy canes
  for garnish

In a large bowl, combine nonfat dry milk, sugar, cocoa powder, powdered creamer and salt. Mix well and set aside. In a large saucepan over high heat, place water. Bring water to a boil and remove from heat. Stir in cocoa mixture and vanilla. Mix well and stir in rum and crème de cacao. Stir until dry ingredients are completely dissolved. To serve, pour into mugs and, if desired, garnish each serving with a mini candy cane.

AMARETTO SOUR

Makes 2 servings

3 oz. amaretto
1 C. lemon lime soda
2 orange slices for garnish

2 maraschino cherries
for garnish

Into 2 lowball glasses, pour 1½ ounces amaretto in each. Add ½ cup lemon lime soda to each glass and mix lightly. Garnish each serving with an orange slice and 1 maraschino cherry.

APPLE-TINIS
Makes 2 servings

2 oz. apple schnapps
2 oz. vodka
2 oz. apple juice

2 slices Granny Smith
apple for garnish

In a cocktail shaker filled with ice, combine apple schnapps, vodka and apple juice. Shake vigorously and strain mixture into chilled martini glasses. Garnish each serving with a slice of Granny Smith apple.

The problem with the world is that everyone is a few drinks behind.

Humphrey Bogart

GARDEN PUNCH

Makes 1 serving

1 oz. light rum
1 oz. dark rum
1 oz. Anejo rum
1 tsp. superfine sugar
3 oz. club soda

1 maraschino cherry for garnish
1 lime wedge for garnish
1 orange slice for garnish
1 pineapple wedge
for garnish

In a cocktail shaker filled with ice, combine light rum, dark rum, Anejo rum and superfine sugar. Shake vigorously and strain mixture into chilled Collins glass. Stir in club soda and garnish with a maraschino cherry, lime wedge, orange slice and pineapple wedge.

GRASSHOPPER
Makes 1 serving

1 oz. green crème de menthe
1 oz. white crème de cacao

¼ C. heavy cream or 1 scoop vanilla ice cream

In a cocktail shaker filled with ice, combine crème de menthe, crème de cacao and heavy cream. Shake vigorously and strain mixture into chilled champagne glass. If using ice cream, blend all ingredients in a blender until well combined.

BIKINI MARTINI
Makes 1 serving

1 oz. coconut flavored rum
¾ oz. vodka

1 oz. pineapple juice
Dash of grenadine syrup

In a cocktail shaker filled with ice, combine coconut flavored rum, vodka, pineapple juice and grenadine syrup. Shake vigorously and strain mixture into chilled martini glass.

CRANBERRY KAMIKAZE
Makes 1 serving

1 oz. vodka
1 oz. orange liqueur

½ oz. lime juice
¼ C. cranberry juice

In a cocktail shaker filled with ice, combine vodka, orange liqueur, lime juice and cranberry juice. Shake vigorously and strain mixture into chilled cocktail glass.

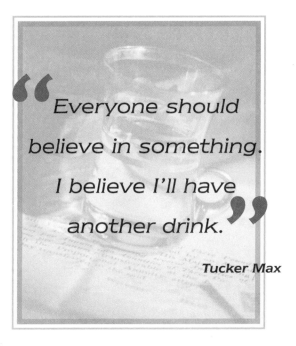

Everyone should believe in something. I believe I'll have another drink.

Tucker Max

PROHIBITION IN THE 1920s

A movement to eliminate saloons and alcoholic beverages from the country in order to reduce crime and corruption, improve health, solve social problems and reduce the tax burden began early in the century. Supported by president Herbert Hoover, prohibition, called "the noble experiment" was written into the 18th Amendment. The Amendment, prohibiting the manufacture, sale and transport of intoxicating liquors, came before the U.S. Senate in 1917 and passed by a one-sided vote after only 13 hours of debate. The House of Representatives accepted the Amendment a few months later with the debate lasting only a day. The state legislatures ratified shortly after and by January of 1919, the necessary 75% of the states had fallen into line and the amendment became part of the Constitution.

UNDERGROUND SPEAKEASIES

Many Americans soon became disenchanted with the Amendment. Underground saloons, called speakeasies, did a booming business. Keeping the saloons supplied became the occupation of rumrunners, bootleggers and beer barons who had to work "around" the law. Inevitably, most of the liquor traffic fell into the hands of gangsters. Alphonse "Scarface Al" Capone of Chicago was one of the most notorious. The gangsters invested their profits in both legitimate and illegitimate businesses. Though Americans had never been particularly law-abiding citizens, statistics on crime in the 20's soared.

THE NEXT DECADE

The 18th Amendment had its share of supporters and detractors. Many believed it was a senseless attempt to enforce the impossible. Basically, those who defended prohibition had it and those who wanted to drink could, and often did. Overall, prohibition was considered a failure, providing underground gangsters their primary source of revenue, thus creating a new set of problems. In 1933, the first year of Franklin D. Roosevelt's administration, prohibition was repealed and liquor, once again, fell under state, rather than a federal, control.

HAWAIIAN PUNCH SLUSH
Makes 8 servings

2 (14 oz.) cans cream
of coconut
2 (6 oz.) cans frozen
lemonade concentrate
1 (46 oz.) can unsweetened
pineapple juice

1 (750 ml.) bottle vodka
2 (1 liter) bottles lemon
lime soda

In a large plastic freezer container, combine cream of coconut, frozen lemonade concentrate, pineapple juice and vodka. Mix until well combined, cover and place in freezer overnight. Remove from freezer 10 minutes before serving. To serve, using an ice cream scooper, divide scoops of the slush mixture into 8 Collins glasses and fill each glass with lemon lime soda.

APRICOT COCKTAIL

Makes 1 serving

Juice of ¼ lemon
Juice of ¼ orange

1½ oz. apricot flavored brandy
1 tsp. gin

Into a cocktail shaker filled with ice, squeeze lemon and orange juice. Add apricot flavored brandy and gin. Shake vigorously and strain mixture into chilled cocktail glass.

> **"I feel sorry for people
> who don't drink.
> When they wake
> up in the morning,
> that's as good as they're
> going to feel all day."**
>
> **Frank Sinatra**

BOURBON COBBLER

Makes 1 serving

2½ oz. bourbon
1 T. lemon juice
2 tsp. grapefruit juice

1½ tsp. almond extract
1 peach slice for garnish

In a cocktail shaker filled with ice, combine bourbon, lemon juice, grapefruit juice and almond extract. Shake vigorously and strain mixture into chilled lowball glass over ice. Garnish with a peach slice.

CARA SPOSA

Makes 1 serving

1 oz. coffee flavored brandy   ½ oz. light cream
1 oz. triple sec

In a cocktail shaker filled with ice, combine coffee flavored brandy, triple sec and light cream. Shake vigorously and strain mixture into chilled cocktail glass.

BULL'S EYE
Makes 1 serving

Ice cubes
1 oz. brandy

2 oz. hard apple cider
Ginger ale

In a lowball glass filled with ice, pour brandy and hard cider. Fill glass with ginger ale and stir lightly.

BOMBAY COCKTAIL
Makes 1 serving

½ oz. dry vermouth
½ oz. sweet vermouth
1 oz. brandy

¼ tsp. anisette
½ tsp. triple sec

In a cocktail shaker filled with ice, combine dry vermouth, sweet vermouth, brandy, anisette and triple sec. Shake vigorously and strain mixture into chilled cocktail glass.

I distrust camels and anyone else who can go a week without a drink.

Joe E. Lewis

WIDOW'S KISS

Makes 1 serving

1 oz. brandy   ½ oz. Benedictine
½ oz. yellow Chartreuse   Dash of bitters

In a cocktail shaker filled with ice, combine brandy, Chartreuse, Benedictine and bitters. Shake vigorously and strain mixture into chilled cocktail glass.

THE MCKENZIE
Makes 1 serving

Juice of ½ lemon
½ tsp. superfine sugar
2 oz. gin

Ice cubes
Club soda
1 lemon slice for garnish

In a cocktail shaker filled with ice, combine lemon juice, sugar and gin. Shake vigorously and strain mixture into highball glass. Add club soda to fill glass and garnish with a lemon slice.

My grandmother is eighty and still doesn't need glasses. Drinks right out of the bottle.

Henny Youngman

BRANDY OLD-FASHIONED
Makes 1 serving

2 dashes Angostura bitters
1 tsp. sugar
2½ oz. brandy

Ice cubes
1 orange slice for garnish

In an old-fashioned glass, combine bitters and sugar. Mix well and add brandy. Stir until sugar is completely dissolved and add ice. Garnish with an orange slice.

MORNING COCKTAIL
Makes 1 serving

1 oz. brandy
1 oz. dry vermouth
¼ tsp. triple sec
¼ tsp. maraschino liqueur

¼ tsp. anisette
2 dashes orange bitters
1 maraschino cherry
for garnish

In a cocktail shaker filled with ice, combine brandy, dry vermouth, triple sec, maraschino, anisette and orange bitters. Shake vigorously and strain mixture into chilled cocktail glass. Garnish with a maraschino cherry.

BLUEBIRD
Makes 1 serving

2 oz. gin
1 oz. triple sec
1 oz. blue curacao

2 dashes bitters
Twist of orange for garnish

In a cocktail shaker filled with ice, combine gin, triple sec, blue curacao and bitters. Shake vigorously and strain mixture into chilled cocktail glass. Garnish with a twist of orange peel.

SOUTHERN MINT JULEP

Makes 1 serving

1 tsp. powdered sugar
2 tsp. water
5 to 6 fresh mint sprigs

Shaved ice
2½ oz. bourbon

In a silver mug or Collins glass, combine powdered sugar, water and 2 mint sprigs. Mix well and crush mint sprigs with a spoon. Fill glass with shaved ice and add bourbon. Stir until well chilled. Add remaining fresh mint sprigs and mix well. Serve immediately.

I never should have switched from Scotch to Martinis.

**The last words
of Humphrey Bogart**

BOURBON WHISKEY BBQ SAUCE
Makes 1 quart

½ onion, chopped
4 cloves garlic, minced
¾ C. bourbon
½ tsp. pepper
½ T. salt
2 C. ketchup

¼ C. tomato paste
⅓ C. cider vinegar
2 T. liquid smoke flavoring
¼ C. Worcestershire sauce
½ C. brown sugar
½ tsp. hot pepper sauce

In a large skillet over medium heat, combine chopped onions, minced garlic and bourbon. Sauté for 10 minutes, until onions are transparent. Add pepper, salt, ketchup, tomato paste, vinegar, liquid smoke flavoring, Worcestershire sauce, brown sugar and hot pepper sauce. Mix until well blended and bring to a boil. Reduce heat to medium low and let simmer for 20 minutes. If smooth sauce is preferred, transfer to a blender or food processor and puree. Use BBQ sauce as a dipping sauce for meat, smothered over steaks, pork or chicken or in recipes calling for barbeque sauce. Store in refrigerator.

ORANGE BRANDY CRANBERRY SAUCE

Makes 4 cups

$^2/_3$ C. grated orange peel
2 C. water
2 C. sugar
$^2/_3$ C. orange juice

1 T. lemon juice
3 C. fresh or frozen
   cranberries
1 T. brandy

In a small saucepan over medium heat, combine grated orange peel and water. Cover pan and bring to a boil. Reduce heat and let simmer for 15 minutes. Drain pan, reserving orange peel and $^1/_3$ cup liquid in saucepan. Add sugar, orange juice and lemon juice. Return to a boil, reduce heat and let simmer for 3 minutes, stirring frequently. Add cranberries and increase heat to medium high. Bring to a boil for 10 minutes, or until cranberries have popped open. Remove from heat and stir in brandy. Pour hot liquid to within $^1/_2$″ of the top of 4½ pint glass jars. Cover tightly and store in refrigerator for up to two weeks.

RUM RAISIN BREAD

Makes 1 (1 pound) loaf

2 T. rum
½ C. raisins
½ C. water
2 C. bread flour
1 T. dry milk powder
2 tsp. brown sugar
1 tsp. salt

2 tsp. butter
2 T. heavy whipping cream
½ tsp. rum extract
1 egg
1 tsp. olive oil
1½ tsp. active dry yeast

In a small bowl, combine rum and raisins. Let stand for 30 minutes or overnight. Drain raisins thoroughly. In the pan of a bread machine, place dry and wet ingredients as recommended by the manufacturer. Set on regular setting and push start. If the machine has a fruit setting, add raisins at the signal. Otherwise, add raisins 5 minutes before the kneading cycle has finished.

CRESCENT WEDGES

Makes 32 servings

2 T. sunflower seeds,
   shelled
1 T. caraway seeds
1 T. sesame seeds
1 (8 oz.) tube refrigerated
   crescent rolls

2 T. Dijon mustard
1 T. bourbon
1 T. honey

Preheat oven to 375°. Grease a large baking sheet and set aside. In a small bowl, combine sunflowers seeds, caraway seeds and sesame seeds. Mix well and set aside. Separate crescent roll dough into 4 rectangles. Place rectangles on prepared baking sheet and cut each rectangle into 8 wedges. In a small bowl, combine mustard, bourbon and honey. Mix well and brush over wedges. Sprinkle seed mixture over wedges and bake in oven for 9 to 14 minutes, until golden brown. Remove from oven and let cool for 5 minutes before serving.

ABOUT GIN

The history of gin dates back to the 17th century, long before the martini gained popularity. In the Netherlands, gin was created by a Dutch chemist, Dr. Sylvius. He was trying to create a medicine that would clean blood for kidney disorders. His concoction, made of neutral grain spirits flavored with juniper, was called "genever", meaning juniper in French.

In 1698, gin was one of the essential products on the French market. Because of French's threat against Holland, William III, who ruled England at the time and was a native of Holland, helped the sale of gin in his country. While French spirits remained expensive in the British market, gin was sold at a very affordable price and was mass-produced. However, gin was often misunderstood as a spirit to induce abortion and became known as "mother's ruin".

Today, gin is distilled from grain and is usually flavored with juniper berries. Most gin is colorless, however some may turn golden due to the aging process in barrels. Though there are many types of gin, dry gin is the most popular. Most gin is sold between 80 and 94 proof. Some popular gin drinks are the Martini, Gin & Tonic and Long Island Iced Tea.

CHICKEN FETTUCCINI
Makes 4 servings

1/3 C. fresh chopped cilantro

2 T. minced garlic

2 T. minced jalapeno peppers

3 T. butter, divided

1/2 C. chicken broth

3 T. tequila

2 T. fresh lime juice

1 1/4 lbs. skinless, boneless chicken breast halves, cubed

3 T. soy sauce

1/4 red onion, sliced

1 red bell pepper, thinly sliced

1/2 yellow bell pepper, thinly sliced

1/2 green bell pepper, thinly sliced

1 1/2 C. heavy whipping cream

1 (16 oz.) pkg. fettuccini pasta, cooked

In a medium saucepan over medium heat, sauté cilantro, minced garlic and minced jalapeno peppers in 2 table-spoons butter for 4 to 5 minutes. Add chicken broth, tequila and lime juice. Bring mixture to a boil, heating until mixture reaches a paste-like consistency. Remove from heat and set aside. In a medium bowl, combine chicken breast cubes and soy sauce. Set aside for 5 minutes. Meanwhile, in a medium skillet over medium high heat, sauté sliced onion and sliced red, yellow and green bell peppers in remaining 1 tablespoon butter. Heat, stirring occasionally, until softened. Add chicken and soy sauce mixture. Mix well and stir in sauce mixture, toss until evenly coated. Bring mixture to a boil. Reduce heat and let simmer until chicken is cooked throughout and sauce has thickened. Add cooked fettuccini and toss until evenly coated. Serve immediately.

TEQUILA LIME CHICKEN
Makes 4 servings

1 C. water
1/3 C. teriyaki sauce
2 T. lime juice
2 tsp. minced garlic
1 tsp. liquid smoke flavoring
1/2 tsp. salt
1/4 tsp. ground ginger
1/4 tsp. tequila
4 skinless, boneless chicken breast halves
1/4 C. mayonnaise
1/4 C. sour cream
1 T. milk
2 tsp. minced sun-dried tomato
1 1/2 tsp. green chile pepper flakes
1 tsp. minced onion flakes
1/4 tsp. dried parsley flakes
1/4 tsp. hot pepper sauce
Pinch of salt
Pinch of dillweed
Pinch of paprika
Pinch of cayenne pepper
Pinch of ground cumin
Pinch of chili powder
Pinch of pepper
1 C. shredded Cheddar Monterey Jack cheese blend
2 C. crushed corn tortilla chips

In a large bowl, combine water, teriyaki sauce, lime juice, minced garlic, liquid smoke flavoring, salt, ground ginger and tequila. Mix well and add chicken breast halves, turning to coat. Cover bowl and let marinate in refrigerator for 2 to 3 hours. To prepare dressing, in a medium bowl, combine mayonnaise, sour cream, milk, minced sun-dried tomato, green chile pepper flakes, minced onion flakes, dried parsley flakes, hot pepper sauce, salt, dillweed, paprika, cayenne pepper, ground cumin, chili powder and pepper. Using a wire whisk, blend mixture until smooth. Cover and chill in refrigerator until ready to use. Preheat broiler. Remove chicken from refrigerator and discard marinade. Place chicken on a broiler pan and place under broiler for 3 to 5 minutes on each side, heating until juices run clean. Place chicken in a 9 x 13″ baking dish and spread dressing mixture over each chicken piece. Top each chicken piece with ¼ cup shredded cheese blend and place under broiler for an additional 2 to 3 minutes, or until cheese is melted. Spread ½ cup crushed chips on each plate and place one chicken breast over chips on each plate. Serve immediately.

> *Claret is the liquor for boys, port for men; but he who aspires to be a hero must drink brandy.*
>
> **Samuel Johnson**

BRANDIED SWEET POTATOES

Makes 12 servings

2 lbs. sweet potatoes	½ C. brandy
½ C. butter	½ tsp. salt
½ C. brown sugar	

Peel sweet potatoes and cut into 2″ pieces. In a large pot of boiling water, cook sweet potatoes until tender. Meanwhile, in a large skillet over medium heat, melt butter. Add brown sugar, brandy and salt, stirring until smooth. Add cooked sweet potatoes and reduce heat to low. Continue to heat until potatoes are heated throughout and well glazed.

ALMOND BAKED BRIE
Makes 8 servings

2 T. butter
1 tsp. crushed garlic
2 T. slivered almonds
1 (8 oz.) can sliced
   mushrooms, drained

1 T. brandy
1 tsp. dried tarragon
1 (8 oz.) wedge Brie
   cheese

Preheat oven to 350°. In a medium saucepan over medium heat, melt butter. Add garlic and slivered almonds, stirring well. Heat until almonds are lightly browned and stir in drained mushrooms, cooking until mushrooms are tender, about 5 minutes. Add brandy and dried tarragon. If necessary, remove coating from Brie cheese. Place Brie on a small baking dish and pour mushroom and almond mixture over cheese. Bake in oven for 20 minutes, or until mixture is bubbly. Serve with various crackers.

CRANBERRY RELISH

Makes 12 servings

1 C. bourbon
¼ C. minced shallots
Zest of 1 orange
1 (12 oz.) pkg. fresh
   cranberries

1 C. sugar
1 tsp. pepper

In a small saucepan over medium heat, combine bourbon, minced shallots and grated orange peel. Bring to a boil, reduce heat and let simmer, stirring occasionally, until mixture has reduced to a syrupy glaze, about 10 minutes. Stir in cranberries and sugar, stirring until sugar is completely dissolved. Reduce heat slightly and continue to simmer until most of the cranberries have burst open, about 10 minutes. Remove from heat and stir in pepper. Transfer mixture to a bowl and let cool to room temperature. Cover and refrigerate until ready to serve.

BOURBON BAKED BEANS

Makes 6 servings

2½ C. dried navy or Great
   Northern beans
1 yellow onion, chopped
¼ C. dark molasses
2 T. brown sugar
1 T. dry mustard
1 T. Worcestershire sauce

½ C. apple cider
2 T. bourbon
¼ C. tomato sauce
½ tsp. salt
¼ tsp. pepper
1 C. water
½ lb. cooked, cubed ham

Rinse beans with water, discarding any dark beans or stones. Place beans in a medium bowl and cover by 2″ water. Let soak overnight and drain. Fill a large saucepan ¾ full with water and place over medium high heat. Bring water to a boil and add drained beans and chopped onion. Return to a boil, reduce heat to medium low, cover and let simmer for 1 to 1½ hours. Remove from heat, drain well and set aside. Preheat oven to 350°. In a large saucepan over medium heat, combine molasses, brown sugar, dry mustard, Worcestershire sauce, apple cider, bourbon, tomato sauce, salt, pepper and water. Bring mixture to a simmer, stirring until brown sugar is completely dissolved. Continue to heat for 1 to 2 minutes. In a large baking dish, combine beans and sauce mixture. If needed, add a little more water. Stir in cubed ham, cover and bake for 35 minutes. Uncover and increase heat to 400°. Continue baking until almost all liquid has absorbed, about 45 to 60 minutes. Remove from oven and serve warm or cool. To reheat, bring chilled beans to room temperature and place in a 375° oven for about 25 minutes.

BRANDY BUTTER
Makes about 1 cup

8 T. butter   2 to 3 T. brandy
½ C. sugar

In a medium mixing bowl, beat butter at medium speed until lightened and fluffy. Add sugar, 1 tablespoon at a time,
and continue to beat until sugar is well incorporated. Add
brandy and beat until well combined. Spoon mixture into a
serving dish and chill in refrigerator until hardened. Serve
as a spread for rolls or topping for potatoes or other veg-
etables.

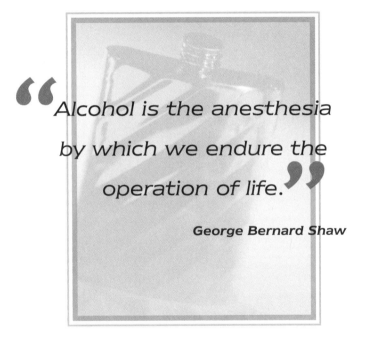

Alcohol is the anesthesia by which we endure the operation of life.

George Bernard Shaw

DERBY POT ROAST

Makes 6 to 8 servings

¼ C. Dijon mustard
½ tsp. ground red pepper, divided
1 tsp. salt
1 (3 lb.) boneless pork loin roast, rolled and tied

1 C. orange marmalade
2 to 3 T. bourbon
2 T. butter

Preheat oven to 325°. In a small bowl, combine mustard, ¼ teaspoon ground red pepper and salt. Mix well and rub over pork loin. Place roast on a rack in a shallow roasting pan. Roast pork in oven for 1 to 1½ hours, or until roast registers between 155° and 160° on a meat thermometer. In a small saucepan over low heat, combine orange marmalade, bourbon, butter and the remaining ¼ teaspoon ground red pepper. Remove roast from oven and slice. Drizzle bourbon sauce over sliced roast.

RUM RUNNERS CHICKEN
Makes 3 to 4 servings

2 tsp. vegetable oil
3 medium onions, thinly
  sliced
6 cloves garlic, chopped
½ C. chicken broth
1 (3 to 3½ lb.) whole chicken
¼ C. dark rum

2 T. apple cider vinegar
½ C. brown sugar
½ tsp. ground cloves
½ tsp. cinnamon
¼ tsp. ground red pepper
1½ tsp. salt

Preheat oven to 350°. In a large skillet over medium heat, heat oil. Stir in sliced onions and chopped garlic and sauté for 8 to 10 minutes. Transfer mixture to a 9 x 13″ baking dish and pour chicken broth over onion mixture. Place chicken over mixture. In a medium bowl, combine rum, apple cider vinegar, brown sugar, ground cloves, cinnamon, ground red pepper and salt. Mix well until a glaze forms. Brush half of the glaze over the chicken and bake in oven for 30 minutes. Drizzle remaining glaze over chicken and bake for an additional 40 to 45 minutes, or until chicken is cooked throughout.

VODKA RIGATONI

Makes 8 servings

1 (7 oz.) jar roasted red peppers	1½ tsp. sugar
¼ lb. chopped prosciutto	1 tsp. salt
2 C. heavy whipping cream	¼ tsp. pepper
1 (28 oz.) can crushed tomatoes in juice	1/8 tsp. red pepper flakes, optional
1 oz. vodka	1 lb. rigatoni pasta
2 T. fresh chopped parsley	1 C. grated Parmesan cheese
2 tsp. garlic powder	¼ C. green peas

Drain roasted pepper, reserving a small amount of the liquid. Cut the peppers into strips. In a large saucepan over medium heat, combine prosciutto, heavy cream, crushed tomatoes in juice, vodka, roasted pepper strips and reserved liquid, parsley, garlic powder, sugar, salt, pepper and, if desired, red pepper flakes. Cover and cook, stirring often, until sauce begins to boil. Reduce heat and let simmer for 30 minutes. Meanwhile, cook rigatoni according to package directions. Drain pasta and transfer to a serving bowl. Add grated Parmesan cheese to sauce mixture and pour over pasta. Mix well and top with peas.

> *I drink when I have occasion, and sometimes when I have no occasion.*
>
> **Cervantes in Don Quixote**

TEQUILA CHICKEN SALAD

Makes 4 servings

8 corn tortillas
4 C. mixed salad greens
½ C. shredded Monterey
  Jack cheese
1 (8 oz.) can black beans,
  rinsed and drained
2 (8 oz.) cans whole kernel
  corn, drained
3 Roma tomatoes, diced
¼ C. diced red onion
1½ C. cooked, chopped
  chicken
2 avocados, peeled
  and cubed

½ C. pitted black olives
¼ C. tequila
2 T. red wine vinegar
2 T. vegetable oil
¼ tsp. hot sauce
¼ tsp. pepper
1 tsp. chili powder
¼ tsp. ground cumin
1 clove garlic, crushed
Juice of 1 lime

Preheat oven to 400°. Place corn tortillas directly on oven rack and bake for 8 minutes, being careful not to burn. Divide salad greens evenly into 4 bowls. Sprinkle shredded cheese, rinsed black beans, drained corn, diced tomatoes, diced red onion, chopped chicken, cubed avocados and black olives over salad greens in each bowl. In a medium bowl, combine tequila, red wine vinegar, vegetable oil, hot sauce, pepper, chili powder, ground cumin, crushed garlic and lime juice. Mix well and drizzle evenly over salad ingredients, tossing lightly. Serve each salad with 2 baked corn tortillas.

GRILLED STEAKS WITH BACON & MUSHROOM SAUCE

Makes 6 servings

6 strips thick bacon, chopped
4 T. butter
1½ lb. white mushrooms, sliced
½ tsp. salt
5 cloves garlic, minced
2 tsp. flour

⅓ C. bourbon
⅔ C. chicken broth
⅓ C. heavy whipping cream
3 T. fresh chopped parsley
Pepper to taste
3 (1½˝ thick) New York strip steaks

In a large saucepan over medium heat, cook chopped bacon until crisp, about 8 minutes. Transfer cooked bacon to paper towels and drain saucepan. Add butter to saucepan over medium high heat. Add sliced mushrooms and salt. Cover and cook until mushrooms are tender, about 6 minutes. Stir in minced garlic and cooked bacon. Increase to high heat and let simmer for 4 minutes, stirring occasionally, until liquid evaporates and mushrooms begin to brown. Sprinkle flour over mushrooms, stirring until flour is completely dissolved. Add bourbon and let simmer about 2 minutes, until most of the bourbon has evaporated. Stir in chicken broth and heavy cream. Season with pepper to taste and let simmer until sauce is thickened. Meanwhile, preheat grill. Place steaks on grate and grill until steaks reach desired doneness. Grill about 4 minutes on each side for medium-rare. Remove steaks from grill and let sit for 5 minutes. Cut steaks into ½˝ thick slices and place on serving plates. Drizzle sauce mixture over steaks and serve.

"What harm in drinking can there be, since punch and life so well agree?

Thomas Blacklock

BRANDY GLAZED HAM
Makes 8 servings

1 (2 lb.) ham, cooked	1 C. raisins
1 C. dry white wine	2 T. butter
1 C. water	2 T. brandy

Preheat oven to 350°. Remove rind from ham and, using a sharp knife, score the surface of the ham in a diamond pattern. Place ham in a baking dish and pour dry white wine and water over ham. Arrange raisins and butter around ham and pour brandy over ham. Bake in oven for about 40 minutes, basting frequently with the pan liquids. When the surface of the ham is crisp and golden, remove from oven and let stand for 10 minutes before slicing.

LEMON VODKA SAUTÉED PORK

Makes 2 servings

2 tsp. olive oil, divided
2 (4 oz.) boned pork chops
Salt and pepper to taste
2 Anjou pears, peeled
   and halved

¼ C. vodka
2 tsp. grated lemon peel
1 T. fresh lemon juice
1 T. fresh chopped
   green onions

In a large skillet over medium heat, heat 1 teaspoon olive oil. Season pork chops with salt and pepper and place in skillet. Sauté on each side for 3 minutes, or until pork is done. Remove from pan and keep warm. Add remaining 1 teaspoon olive oil to pan and place pears in pan, cut side down. Sauté for 2 minutes on each side. Remove pears from pan and keep warm. To skillet, add vodka, grated lemon peel, lemon juice, green onions and salt and pepper to taste. Cook over medium heat for 1 minute. To serve, place 1 pork chop and 1 pear on each plate and drizzle sauce over each serving.

WHISKEY MARINATED SALMON

Makes 4 servings

1 (1 lb.) fresh salmon filet
1 tsp. grated lemon peel
¼ C. lemon juice
¼ C. whiskey

1 T. vegetable oil
¼ tsp. dry mustard
1 clove garlic, crushed
1 T. dried rosemary

Thoroughly rinse salmon and pat dry. Cut filet into 4 pieces. In a shallow dish, combine grated lemon peel, lemon juice, whiskey, vegetable oil, dry mustard and crushed garlic. Set aside half of the marinade mixture. Add salmon pieces and turn until coated in remaining marinade mixture. Cover and let marinate in refrigerator for 1 to 1½ hours. Remove salmon from refrigerator and drain. Preheat broiler. Place salmon pieces on a broiler pan and brush with reserved marinade mixture and rub with dried rosemary. Place salmon 4″ under broiler for 5 minutes. Turn salmon over and brush with marinade. Place under broiler for an additional 5 minutes. Salmon is done when it flakes easily with a fork.

CHICKEN FETTUCCINE WITH ROSEMARY SAUCE

Makes 6 servings

3 T. butter
2 large onions, finely diced
¼ C. brandy
¼ C. flour
1 tsp. salt
1 tsp. paprika
1 T. fresh chopped rosemary
Pepper to taste

2 C. chicken broth
1¼ C. sour cream
½ C. milk
½ lb. cooked, cubed chicken
1 lb. fettuccine
1 large avocado, peeled and diced

In a large saucepan over medium heat, melt butter. Add finely diced onions and sauté until well cooked. Add brandy and let simmer until liquid is almost all absorbed. Gradually stir in flour and cook until thickened. Add salt, paprika, chopped rosemary and pepper. Heat for 2 minutes, stirring occasionally, and add chicken broth. Bring mixture to a gentle boil for 3 minutes. Remove from heat and gradually stir in sour cream and milk. Add cooked, chopped chicken and return to low heat. Let mixture simmer for 15 minutes. Meanwhile, in a large pot of lightly salted boiling water, cook fettuccine until al dente. Right before serving, mix diced avocado into sauce. Divide cooked pasta evenly onto 6 plates and top with sauce mixture.

DELICIOUS BEEF STROGANOFF

Makes 4 servings

¼ C. olive oil
1 (1¼ lb.) beef tenderloin steak, cut into 2 x ½″ strips
2 T. butter
3 large shallots, finely chopped

1 T. paprika
⅔ C. thinly sliced button mushrooms
2 T. white wine vinegar
3 T. brandy
1 C. chicken broth
6 T. sour cream

In a large skillet over high heat, heat oil. When oil is very hot, add beef tenderloin strips in batches and fry for 3 to 5 minutes, stirring constantly, until lightly browned. Remove meat from pan, set aside and keep warm. Add butter and chopped shallots to pan and sauté for 2 minutes, until softened. Stir in paprika and heat for 45 seconds. Stir in sliced button mushrooms and continue to heat until mixture is dry. Add vinegar and heat for an additional 1 minute, until almost all liquid is absorbed. Add brandy and cook until liquid has reduced by half. Stir in chicken broth and heat until reduced by half again. Finally, stir in sour cream and return cooked meat to pan. Mix until heated throughout and serve.

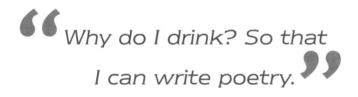

"Why do I drink? So that I can write poetry."

Jim Morrison

ABOUT RUM

In the early 17th century, British settlers in the West Indies cultivated sugar cane plantations as the foundation of their economic growth. A capital-intense business was created and the need for labor was high, creating a demand for slaves. From New England, a skipper would travel to West Africa with a cargo of rum. Once there, he would exchange rum for many slaves and head to the West Indies. There he would trade the slaves for molasses and return to New England, Connecticut and New York where the molasses would be distilled into rum. The skippers would reap great profits following this pattern, which became known as the triangle trade.

Sugarcane is the basic ingredient of rum. The sugarcane is boiled down and the remaining residue is spun until it crystallizes. The crystallized form is separated from the congealed form, known as molasses. The molasses is then boiled and mixed with water and yeast. The mixture is distilled and aged in oak casks.

There are two basic types of rum: light and dark. Dark rum ages longer than light rum; anywhere from 3 to 12 years. Caramel is added to dark rum, which has a richer aroma and flavor than light rum. This type of rum is mainly produced in the tropical islands of Jamaica, Haiti and Martinique. Light rum requires no longer than 6 months of aging in the oak casks and is traditionally made in the southern Caribbean Islands of Puerto Rico and Trinidad.

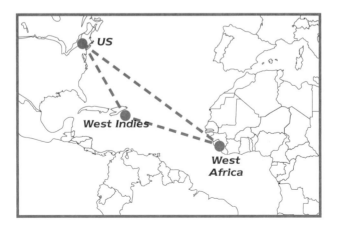

"*Give an Irishman lager for a month and he's a dead man. An Irishman's stomach is lined with copper, and the beer corrodes it. But whiskey polishes the copper and is the saving of him.*"

Mark Twain

BREAD PUDDING IN WHISKEY SAUCE
Makes 12 servings

6 eggs, lightly beaten
3 C. sugar, divided
4 C. milk
1 C. heavy whipping cream
1 T. vanilla
½ T. cinnamon

1 (1 lb.) loaf bread,
  cut into 1″ cubes
½ C. golden raisins
¾ C. butter
¾ C. corn syrup
½ C. whiskey

Preheat oven to 300°. In a medium bowl, combine eggs and 1½ cups sugar. Mix well and add milk, heavy cream, vanilla and cinnamon. Blend mixture until smooth. In a 9″ square baking dish, arrange bread cubes across bottom of dish. Sprinkle golden raisins over bread cubes. Pour cream mixture over bread and raisins, allowing bread to become saturated. Bake in oven for 45 minutes, or until lightly browned. To prepare sauce, in a medium saucepan over low heat, combine remaining 1½ cups sugar, butter and corn syrup. Heat until warmed, remove from heat and blend in whiskey. Divide bread pudding into 12 bowls and drizzle warm whiskey sauce over each serving.

MARGARITA PARTY CAKE
Makes 1 (10″) bundt cake

1 (18¼ oz.) pkg. orange
  cake mix
1 (3½ oz.) pkg. instant
  vanilla pudding mix
4 eggs
½ C. vegetable oil
²/₃ C. water

¼ C. lemon juice
¼ C. plus 1 T. tequila,
  divided
4 T. triple sec, divided
1 C. powdered sugar
2 T. lime juice

Preheat oven to 350°. Grease and flour a 10″ bundt cake pan. In a large mixing bowl, combine orange cake mix, vanilla pudding mix, eggs, vegetable oil, water, lemon juice, ¼ cup tequila and 2 tablespoons triple sec. Beat at high speed for 2 minutes. Pour batter into prepared bundt pan and bake in oven for 45 to 50 minutes, or until a toothpick inserted in center of cake comes out clean. Remove from oven and let cool in pan for 10 minutes. To prepare glaze, in a small bowl, combine powdered sugar, remaining 1 tablespoon tequila, remaining 2 tablespoons triple sec and lime juice. Mix until smooth. Drizzle glaze over cake while still warm.

CRANBERRY BRANDY COOKIES

Makes 2 dozen

½ C. butter, softened
½ C. brown sugar
½ C. sugar
1 egg
1 T. brandy

1½ C. flour
½ tsp. baking soda
¾ C. white baking chips
1 C. dried cranberries

Preheat oven to 375°. Grease two baking sheets and set aside. In a large bowl, cream together butter, brown sugar and sugar, mixing until smooth. Add egg and brandy and mix well. In a separate bowl, combine flour and baking soda. Add flour mixture to creamed mixture and mix until well combined. Fold in white baking chips and dried cranberries. Drop dough by tablespoonfuls onto prepared baking sheets. Bake in oven for 8 to 10 minutes. Remove from oven while cookies are still soft. Let cool for 1 minute on baking sheets before transferring to wire racks to cool completely.

DIVINE AMARETTO TORTE

Makes 1 (8˝) cake

1 (18¼ oz.) pkg. yellow
cake mix
2 C. liquid amaretto flavored
creamer, divided
1¼ C. amaretto, divided
3 eggs
⅓ C. vegetable oil

1 (3½ oz.) pkg. instant
vanilla pudding mix
2 C. whipped topping
4 (1½ oz.) bars chocolate
covered toffee, chopped
1 (1½ oz.) bar chocolate,
melted
½ C. sliced almonds

Preheat oven to 325°. Grease and flour three 8˝ cake pans. In a medium bowl, combine yellow cake mix, 1 cup amaretto flavored creamer, 1 cup amaretto, eggs and vegetable oil, mixing until well blended. Divide batter evenly into prepared pans. Bake in oven for 15 minutes, being careful not to overbake. Remove from oven and let cool completely. To prepare filling, in a medium bowl, combine vanilla pudding mix, remaining ¼ cup amaretto and remaining 1 cup amaretto flavored creamer. Mix well and set aside for

5 minutes, until thickened. Fold in whipped topping and crushed chocolate toffee bars. To assemble cake, place one cake layer on a serving platter. Spread 1/3 of the topping mixture over cake and top with another layer. Spread another 1/3 of the topping over cake and top with final cake layer. Spread remaining topping over top of cake, but not the sides. Drizzle melted chocolate over cake and sprinkle sliced almonds over cake.

"I have taken more out of alcohol than alcohol has taken out of me."

Winston Churchill

GOLDEN RUM CAKE
Makes 1 bundt cake

1 C. chopped walnuts
1 (18¼ oz.) pkg. yellow cake mix
1 (3½ oz.) pkg. instant vanilla pudding mix
4 eggs

¾ C. water, divided
½ C. vegetable oil
1 C. dark rum, divided
½ C. butter
1 C. sugar

Preheat oven to 325°. Grease and flour a 10˝ bundt cake pan and sprinkle chopped walnuts evenly over bottom of pan. In a large bowl, combine yellow cake mix and vanilla pudding mix. Add eggs, ½ cup water, vegetable oil and ½ cup rum. Mix well and pour batter over walnuts in pan. Bake in oven for 60 minutes, or until a toothpick inserted in center of cake comes out clean. Remove from oven and let sit for 10 minutes. Invert cake onto a serving platter. Meanwhile, to prepare glaze, in a small saucepan over medium heat, combine butter, remaining ¼ cup water and sugar. Bring mixture to a boil for 5 minutes. Remove from heat and stir in remaining ½ cup rum. Brush glaze over top and sides of cake.

PINA COLADA CAKE
Makes 1 bundt cake

1 (18¼ oz.) pkg. yellow cake mix

1 (3½ oz.) pkg. instant vanilla pudding mix

1 (14 oz.) can cream of coconut

½ C plus 2 T. rum, divided

⅓ C. vegetable oil

4 eggs

1 (8 oz.) can crushed pineapple, drained

Preheat oven to 350°. Grease and flour a 10″ bundt cake pan. In a large mixing bowl, combine yellow cake mix, vanilla pudding mix, ½ cup cream of coconut, ½ cup rum, vegetable oil and eggs. Beat at medium speed for 2 minutes. Fold in drained pineapple. Pour mixture into prepared pan. Bake in oven for 50 to 55 minutes. Remove from oven and let cool for 10 minutes. Invert cake onto a serving platter. Using a wooden skewer, poke holes 1″ apart over surface of cake. In a medium bowl, combine remaining cream of coconut and remaining 2 tablespoons rum. Drizzle over cake. Chill in refrigerator until ready to serve.

RUM SNACKERS
Makes 4 dozen

1 (11 oz.) pkg. chocolate
    wafer cookies, finely
    crushed
1½ C. finely chopped pecans

½ C. light corn syrup
¼ C. rum
½ C. powdered sugar

In a large bowl, combine crushed chocolate wafer cookies
and chopped pecans. Mix well and stir in corn syrup and
rum, mixing until well combined. In a shallow bowl, place
powdered sugar. Roll pecan mixture into 1˝ balls and roll
in powdered sugar until evenly coated. Store in an airtight
container at room temperature.

APRICOT BREAD PUDDING
Makes 12 servings

1 (1 lb.) loaf Italian bread,
   torn into 1″ pieces
2 C. warm water
3 eggs
1 C. heavy whipping cream
½ C. finely chopped dried
   apricots

1 tsp. vanilla
¾ C. sugar
1 tsp. salt
½ tsp. cinnamon
½ C. powdered sugar
2 T. apricot flavored brandy

Preheat oven to 350°. Grease an 8″ square baking dish and set aside. In a large bowl, toss together bread pieces and water, mixing until bread is soaked. In a small mixing bowl, beat eggs at medium speed and add heavy cream. Beat for 1 minute and add to soaked bread. Fold in chopped apricots, vanilla, sugar, salt and cinnamon, mixing until well combined. Transfer mixture to prepared baking dish and bake in oven for 60 to 65 minutes, or until pudding is puffy and firm in the center. Meanwhile, in a small bowl, combine powdered sugar and apricot brandy, stirring until smooth. Remove pudding from oven and, while still warm, drizzle glaze mixture over bread pudding.

MOCHA MUDSLIDE BROWNIES

Makes 3 dozen

²/₃ C. butter
4 (1 oz.) squares unsweetened chocolate, chopped
3 eggs
1½ C. sugar
¼ C. coffee flavored liqueur

2 T. Irish cream liqueur
2 T. vodka
2 C. flour
½ tsp. baking powder
¾ C. chopped walnuts

Preheat oven to 350°. In a double boiler over medium high heat, melt butter and chopped chocolate, stirring frequently, until melted and smooth. Remove from heat and set aside to cool. In a large mixing bowl, beat eggs and sugar for 5 minutes. Fold in melted chocolate, coffee liqueur, Irish cream liqueur and vodka. In a medium bowl, combine flour and baking powder. Fold flour mixture and chopped walnuts into butter mixture. Mix well and spread batter evenly into a lightly greased 9 x 13″ baking dish. Bake in oven for 25 minutes, or until brownies pull away from edges of the pan. Remove from oven and let cool.

"*No poems can please for long or live that are written by water-drinkers.*"

Horace

GLAZED AMARETTO CAKE

Makes 1 (10˝) bundt cake

1 (18¼ oz.) pkg. yellow
  cake mix
4 eggs
1 (5 oz.) pkg. instant vanilla
  pudding mix
½ C. plus 2 T. amaretto,
  divided

½ C. water
½ C. vegetable oil
¼ tsp. almond extract
1 C. powdered sugar, sifted

Preheat oven to 350°. Grease and flour a 10˝ bundt cake
pan. In a large bowl, combine yellow cake mix, eggs, instant vanilla pudding mix, water, vegetable oil and 2 table-
spoons amaretto. Mix well and pour batter into prepared
pan. Bake in oven for 40 to 45 minutes, or until a toothpick
inserted in center of cake comes out clean. Meanwhile,
to prepare glaze, in a medium bowl, combine powdered
sugar and remaining ½ cup amaretto. Blend until smooth,
adding more amaretto if needed. Remove cake from oven
and poke holes in surface of cake. While still warm, drizzle
amaretto glaze over cake. Let cake cool at least 2 hours
before serving.

CHERRY CHOCOLATE FONDUE
Makes 6 servings

2 C. milk chocolate chips
3 T. heavy whipping cream
2 T. cherry brandy

1 T. strong brewed coffee
1/8 tsp. cinnamon

In a fondue pot or small saucepan over a low flame, combine milk chocolate chips, heavy cream, cherry brandy, strong brewed coffee and cinnamon. Heat until melted, stirring frequently. Serve immediately with fresh cut fruits or cake squares for dipping.

ABOUT BOURBON

Bourbon is America's only native spirit and was first created in Kentucky during the 18th century. The spring water that flowed from the cold, clear limestone was perfect for creating Bourbon whiskey that is smooth and sweet. Today, more than 80 percent of the world's bourbon is still produced in Kentucky. Many of the state's distilleries safely guard generations-old recipes for the unique blend.

Bourbon is distilled from a mash of grain that must contain no less than 51 percent corn, according to federal law. Barley, wheat or rye are also added to the mix. The signature aging process of bourbon helps enhance the rich amber color and characteristic sweetness of the liquor. Bourbon is aged in new white oak barrels, which are charred to caramelize the natural sugars in the wood and bring them to the surface. By law, bourbon must be aged at least 2 years, though most are aged between 4 and 12 years. State law also requires that bourbon cannot be distilled above 160 proof and must be bottled at no less than 80 proof.

ABOUT BRANDY

Distilled from fermented fruit, brandy has long been enjoyed as an after-dinner drink. Brandy is produced in a number of countries and is usually bottled at 80 proof. There are many types of brandy, including those distilled directly from fruits, such as cherries, pears and raspberries. There are also fruit-flavored brandies, which are brandy based liqueurs flavored with blackberries, peaches, apricots, cherries and other fruits.

Cognac is a fine brandy known for its smoothness and heavy scent. This type of brandy is produced only in the Cognac region of France. Armagnac is much like Cognac, but has a richer taste. It is produced only in the Armagnac region of France. Most American brandies, which are typically light and smooth, are distilled, aged, blended and bottled in California. Germany also holds a tradition of creating fine brandy, which is created in both pot and continuous stills.

PUMPKIN CHEESECAKE

Makes 1 (10″) cake

1½ C. graham cracker crumbs
½ C. butter, melted
1¼ C. sugar, divided
1 (12 oz.) pkg. cream
    cheese, softened
4 medium eggs
1 (14 oz.) can pumpkin puree

2½ tsp. ground ginger
1 T. cinnamon
½ tsp. nutmeg
¼ tsp. ground cloves
⅓ C. brandy
Whipped topping

Preheat oven to 350°. In a medium bowl, combine graham cracker crumbs, melted butter and ¼ cup sugar. Mix well and press mixture evenly into bottom and 2″ up sides of a 10″ springform pan. Bake in oven for 10 minutes. Remove from oven and reduce oven temperature to 325°. In a medium mixing bowl, beat cream cheese and remaining 1 cup sugar until lightened and fluffy. Add eggs, one at a time, beating well after each addition. Add pumpkin puree, ground ginger, cinnamon, nutmeg, ground cloves and brandy. Pour mixture evenly into crust and return to oven for 50 to 60 minutes, or until center of cake has risen. Turn off oven and let cheesecake cool in oven. When cold, top cheesecake with whipped topping and serve. Store in refrigerator.

"*A man may acquire a taste for wine or brandy, and so lose his love for water, but should we not pity him.*"

Henry David Thoreau

MISSISSIPPI CHOCOLATE COFFEE CAKE

Makes 10 servings

2 C. flour
1 tsp. baking soda
Pinch of salt
1¾ C. strong brewed coffee
¼ C. bourbon
5 (1 oz.) squares unsweetened chocolate

1 C. plus 4½ T. butter,
divided
2 C. sugar
2 large eggs, lightly beaten
1 tsp. vanilla
¾ C. chocolate chips

Preheat oven to 350°. Lightly grease a 9″ round cake pan and line with parchment paper. Into a medium mixing bowl, sift flour, baking soda and salt. In a double boiler over medium heat, combine strong brewed coffee, bourbon, unsweetened chocolate squares and 1 cup butter. Heat, stirring frequently, until completely melted and smooth. Remove from heat and stir in sugar. Let mixture cool for 3 minutes before transferring to a mixing bowl. Add flour mixture, 1 cup at a time, to chocolate mixture in mixing bowl. Beat at medium speed for 1 minute and add eggs and vanilla. Pour mixture into prepared cake pan and bake in oven for 1½ hours, or until a toothpick inserted in center of cake comes out clean. Remove from oven and let cake cool completely. Meanwhile, in a double boiler over low heat, combine chocolate chips and remaining 4½ table-spoons butter. Heat, stirring frequently, until melted and smooth. Remove cake from pan and place on a serving platter. Spread chocolate frosting over top and sides of cake. Chill in refrigerator until ready to serve. Store left-overs in refrigerator.

BUTTERSCOTCH CRUNCH ICE CREAM
Makes 1 quart

¼ C. heavy whipping cream
4 T. butter
2½ C. brown sugar, divided
½ tsp. salt
1 T. Scotch whiskey

2 tsp. vanilla, divided
3 C. milk
1 vanilla bean, split
9 large egg yolks

Lightly grease a 9 x 13″ baking dish and set aside. In a medium heavy saucepan over medium high heat, combine heavy cream, butter, 1¼ cups brown sugar and salt. Bring mixture to a boil, stirring often. When mixture reaches 285° on a candy thermometer, remove from heat and carefully stir in whiskey and 1 teaspoon vanilla. Carefully pour mixture into prepared pan and spread evenly with a greased spatula. Set aside to cool and harden. Once cooled, break into chunks and place in a food processor. Process on high until butterscotch is broken to the size of corn kernels. To prepare ice cream, in a medium heavy saucepan over medium heat, place milk. Scrape seeds from vanilla bean and add seeds and pod to milk. Bring to a simmer. Fill a large bowl with ice. Meanwhile, in a medium bowl, combine remaining 1 cup brown sugar, egg yolks and remaining 1 teaspoon vanilla. Slowly pour some of the hot milk mixture into the egg yolks mixture. Stir lightly and return mixture to milk mixture over medium heat. Stir until slightly thickened and mixture coats the back of a wooden spoon. Pour mixture into a medium bowl and set bowl inside bowl of ice, stirring until mixture is cooled. Chill in refrigerator until very cold and strain mixture into cream container of an ice cream machine. Follow manufacturer's directions. When ice cream is almost frozen, fold in butterscotch pieces. Return to freezer until hardened.

STRAWBERRY PARFAITS

Makes 6 servings

3 C. heavy whipping cream
1½ C. chopped strawberries
¾ C. slivered almonds, toasted*
9 macaroon cookies, crushed

⅓ C. brandy
3 egg whites
¾ C. superfine sugar
½ tsp. baking powder
Whipped topping
Fresh mint sprigs for garnish

In a medium mixing bowl, beat heavy cream at high speed until soft peaks form and set aside. In a small bowl, toss together chopped strawberries, toasted almonds, crushed macaroons and brandy. Set aside for 10 minutes. In a large mixing bowl, beat egg whites at high speed until stiff peaks form. Add sugar and baking powder and continue to beat until mixture is shiny. Fold in whipped cream and strawberry mixture. Divide mixture evenly into 6 parfait glasses and chill in refrigerator until ready to serve. Before serving, top with dollops of whipped topping and fresh mint sprigs for garnish.

* To toast, place slivered almonds in a single layer on a baking sheet. Bake at 350° for approximately 10 minutes or until almonds are golden brown.

INDEX

S P I R I T S